Gol as a Hobby

BY ROBERT HILBLE &
GABRIELE LANGFELDT-FELDMAN

TRANSLATED BY U. ERICH FRIESE

SAVE-OUR-PLANET SERIES

Distributed in the UNITED STATES to the Pet Trade
by T.F.H. Publications, Inc., One T.F.H. Plaza, Nep-
tune City, NJ 07753; distributed in the UNITED
STATES to the Bookstore and Library Trade by
National Book Network, Inc. 4720 Boston Way,
Lanham MD 20706; in CANADA to the Pet Trade by
H & L Pet Supplies Inc., 27 Kingston Crescent,
Kitchener, Ontario N2B 2T6; Rolf C. Hagen Ltd.,
3225 Sartelon Street, Montreal 382 Quebec; in
CANADA to the Book Trade by Macmillan of Canada
(A Division of Canada Publishing Corporation), 164
Commander Boulevard, Agincourt, Ontario M1S
3C7; in ENGLAND by T.F.H. Publications, PO Box
15, Waterlooville PO7 6BQ; in AUSTRALIA AND
THE SOUTH PACIFIC by T.F.H. (Australia), Pty.
Ltd., Box 149, Brookvale 2100 N.S.W., Australia; in
NEW ZEALAND by Brooklands Aquarium Ltd., 5
McGiven Drive, New Plymouth, RD1 New Zealand;
in the PHILIPPINES by Bio-Research, 5 Lippay
Street, San Lorenzo Village, Makati, Rizal; in SOUTH
AFRICA by Multipet Pty. Ltd., P.O. Box 35347,
Northway, 4065, South Africa. Published by T.F.H.
Publications, Inc. Manufactured in the United States
of America by T.F.H. Publications, Inc.

Contents

Preface 6
History of the Goldfish 11
Goldfish Varieties 13
Accommodation 21
Buying Your Goldfish......................................51
Care and Maintenance....................................55
The Goldfish Diet 62
Behavior 67
Diseases 82
Index..98

Photo & Art Credits: David Alderton, David Axelrod, Dr. Herbert R. Axelrod, Mark Batell, K. Cole, Jaroslav Elias, Frickhinger, Michael Gilroy, B. Greger, P. Hodgkinson, Hawaiian Marine Imports, Burkhard Kahl, Robert Mertlich, Hugh Nicholas, J.R. Quinn, Fred Rosenzweig, Dieter Schmidtke, Vince Serbin, Dr. D. Untergasser, L. Wischnath, Yokoyama

Facing Page: The massive head growth and over all body of this oranda are undergoing a color change.

A beautiful red and white telescope-eye with excellent conformation and finnage.

Preface

For many people the common goldfish is the very first love in a long line of friendships with these fascinating pets. The goldfish is often at the very beginning of a subdued or stormy relationship, either fervently desired or tolerated as an educational tool. There is no other fish as popular as *Carassius auratus*, the goldfish.

Therefore, if everyone knows all about goldfish, why write a book about them? Goldfish are the same as many other things in life in

Goldfish are available in various shapes, sizes, and colors. The common goldfish shown here is often a candidate for the beginner's first goldfish aquarium.

that we think we know all about them because they are inexpensive and available everywhere. Nobody gives them much thought anymore but the goldfish deserve better. Although their value is rather low, the goldfish are still surrounded by an aura of fascination of days gone by. Whenever or wherever we see a goldfish it immediately catches our attention. This phenomenon has been cleverly utilized by restaurants and other businesses, which often display goldfish in large tanks or in attractively landscaped outdoor ponds. Both adults and children alike have succumbed unconsciously to the dreamy charm of goldfish in a summery landscape. Children have always been fascinated by goldfish. Many parents have taken advantage of this by using goldfish as a learning device in teaching their children responsible pet care.

Common goldfish are relatively hardy and inexpensive. From a financial point of view a common goldfish's demise is not very tragic. In the beginning losses among goldfish are high. This should not be interpreted as inadequate attention on the part of the hobbyist, but more likely the lack of basic

The veiltail has long, flowing fins and is a favorite among advanced goldfish fanciers.

aquarium knowledge. A common beginners' mistake is overfeeding. They often allow uneaten food to lie on the aquarium bottom where it will slowly decay and later cause harmful pollution. In most cases, these goldfish tanks aren't even filtered. It's even rumored that goldfish have spent the night in the

comprehensive guide on the care and maintenance of goldfish.

Our extensive group of goldfish enthusiasts included Robert Hilble, a famous fish breeder and goldfish expert. I met him for the first time when I was buying goldfish for my garden pond. From the very beginning I was

A well-balanced red ranchu with a solid, compact body.

beds of their young owners—securely covered—and of course have not survived! This goes to show the outlandish extremes that some of the more young, uninformed goldfish enthusiasts practice. While this is undoubtedly an isolated and bizarre case, the lack of knowledge about the vital functions and actual requirements of goldfish are not. In this book, the authors would like to provide the reader with an easy to understand and

impressed by his enthusiasm for his work. He's been involved with fishes from his early childhood days, when his father was actively breeding trout and carp. Robert Hilble, an active fish breeder for more than 12 years, had more than enough knowledge and experience to answer my many, many questions. He enjoyed the selling and breeding of fishes, and generously gave advice and other helpful aquarium tips. He always had a solution for my various fish and pond problems. After a few extensive discussions, it became obvious that not only did I have a lot of questions, but, logically, my problems were also very similar to those of other people. For the most part, these questions always revolved around keeping

opinions is presented here in some detail. Hopefully, it will make your hobby of keeping goldfish a more pleasant, relaxing, and enjoyable recreational activity.

All details in this book have been carefully checked. At the time of publication they represented the latest

Lionheads, similar in appearance to ranchus, are sometimes confused with them.

goldfish in outdoor ponds, pond construction, water quality, and diseases. In our talks we noticed that I, the beginner, was confronted by problems that are alien to an expert fish breeder who, because of his professional operation and sophisticated equipment, never encounters the many difficulties that the beginning aquarist has to deal with because of his limited resources.

The result of this liberal exchange of ideas, views, and

scientific findings. Yet, since there is a continuous accumulation of new knowledge and past findings, anybody using this material must make sure that the details referred to in this text haven't yet been superseded by newer information. For instance, "treating animals" means consulting a veterinarian and reading packing slips, as well as following directions-of-use for medications and other products.

History of the Goldfish

The ancestor of the goldfish is the Prussian or Gibel Carp, *Carassius auratus gibelio*. The Gibel Carp, that is the goldfish, belongs to the large family of carp-like fishes, one of the largest and most widely distributed groups of freshwater fishes in the world. It occurs in Eurasia, Africa, and North America. Fossil records of these fish date back to the Tertiary where they were originally warm-water fishes. The first color varieties among goldfish were accidental products. They originated from natural genetic mutants which were then selectively line-bred.

The first known successful breeding occurred in China, during the Sung Dynasty (about 1000 A.D.), although goldfish were previously mentioned in early Chinese poetry as far back as 800 B.C. Two districts in China—Che Chian Chen and Chian Su Chen—are still at odds with each other as to where the first red goldfish was bred.

At that time colored fishes were very rare and valuable, and keeping them was a privilege reserved for nobility and the rich. The preciousness and desirability of the goldfish may have been the reason they were brought to Japan at about 1500, and from there on to Europe in 1611. Similarly, the first goldfish were shipped from Japan to America in 1876. At that time it was very difficult to keep freshwater fishes alive during sea voyages which would last many weeks. There was no filtration equipment available for purifying the water, and since the fish containers were located on deck, there was an ever-present danger that salt water would injure them. Only a few fishes survived such ordeals. Yet, those that survived often commanded a high price, making such risky ventures worthwhile.

Nowadays, these sort of problems no longer exist, since fishes are now shipped on board airplanes which can reach any part of the world within a few hours. Here, in our part of the world, the goldfish was so popular that it was already being bred during the last century. Long-tailed goldfish were first shown by the breeder Paul Matte in 1880, and were a huge success at all shows. At the beginning of 1900, there were about 30 German goldfish breeders that were held in high professional esteem. After World War II the Italians penetrated the market because of the the advantage of a favorable climate. Their goldfish grew more rapidly

Facing Page: For thousands of years the goldfish has been portrayed in famous paintings and sculptures.

A nicely shaped calico oranda with a lovely metallic sheen.

and reached marketable sizes in relatively short periods of time. This, of course, had a profound effect on prices. Since that time professional goldfish breeding in Germany has been insignificant, but to this day there are still inquiries about the long-tailed varieties bred by Matte. These strains could not be bred again and they have long become extinct. The modern-day goldfish favorite among German aquarists is the Oranda. This variety has gained much popularity with its beautifully flowing finnage and unusual facial expression.

Goldfish Varieties

There are so many different strains and varieties of goldfish that the actual name "goldfish" can really only be applied to the common goldfish. Below are descriptions that explain the different varieties, their care and maintenance, and what

yellow, gold, red and red-and-white. Juvenile fish are blackish brown and normally obtain the final adult colors at an age of 1 to 2 years. Black patches or black fin margins look very attractive, but they often disappear in adult fish. The common goldfish is a

These adult comets display attractive coloration. The juvenile comet is a dull brown or black in color.

location they are most suitable for, whether it be the outdoor pond or an indoor aquarium. There are, of course, minimum requirements in regard to tank and pond maintenance, but these are discussed in detail in a separate chapter of this book.

THE COMMON GOLDFISH

In body shape the goldfish most closely resembles the Prussian Carp or Gibel. It is relatively slender, with short fins, and is bred in several colors, including white, silver,

favorite among children and pond owners. It's inexpensive and hardy, and usually gets along well with other fishes. It can be kept in ponds as well as outdoor and indoor aquariums.

COMET

The Comet is very similar to the common goldfish in body shape, but the tail is longer and deeply forked. Its constant activity makes it a favorite among pond owners. The most attractive is the red-white variety (Sarasa Comet). It too is rather hardy and ideally suited for garden ponds. The pond must have a water depth of at least 3 feet, so it doesn't completely freeze during the winter. Comets can also be kept in aquariums, but such tanks must be sufficiently large.

SHUBUNKIN

Shubunkins incorporate all possible goldfish colors, although a nicely developed blue is highly desirable. These very attractive fish have the body shape and finnage of a Comet. It's important that they show well-developed markings of a black dotted pattern extending onto the fins. The background is multi-colored with shades of white, gold, red, brown, silver and blue. Sometimes Shubunkins have a rather long tail fin that is rounded off. A charming pond fish which, because of its attractive coloration, is often kept in aquariums. This fish must be given adequate swimming space.

FANTAIL

The Fantail has a compact, roundish body shape. The back is bent downward quite acutely and the head is pointed. The fins are relatively long and the tail fin is split and deeply forked. The anal fin is paired. The scales have a metallic sheen. Coloration is usually red or red and white. It is recommended that fantails, like all other compressed bodied, slow-

A beautiful group of calico fantails. Fantails and ryukins are basically the same fish.

This pair of red and white ryukins are not suitable for outdoor living and are more comfortable in the confines of the home aquarium.

moving goldfish varieties, should not be kept outdoors. These fish are quite sensitive to cooler water temperatures. Moreover, because of their slow movements they are easy prey for all sorts of enemies. Fantails are far more effectively displayed in indoor tanks where they are also better protected against injuries.

TOSAKIN (CURLY-TAILED FANTAIL)

This variety is a further development of the Fantail, and is distinguishable from the original strain by a tail fin which is bent forward quite gracefully. This fish is most effectively displayed in an indoor vat or pond, because the tail fin is best seen from above. It shouldn't be kept outdoors because it is quite sensitive. It's very rare and valuable.

VEILTAIL

This form epitomizes the Veiltail goldfish. The anal and tail fins are paired, and like the median fins they are long and elegantly flowing when the fish swims. They're available in all the goldfish colors. The Veiltail is also sensitive to extremely low water temperatures, and there is always a real risk that the delicate fins may be damaged. Another immediate threat is any fast-swimming or aggressive fishes that may pick at their fins. Fishes of this type should always be avoided. The Veiltail is a wonderfully pleasing sight when displayed in the aquarium.

TELESCOPE-EYE

Telescope-eyes are usually fantails or veiltails with strongly protruding laterally extended eyes. Development of the eyes takes about 2 years, and only then can it be ascertained as to whether there is a fish conforming to the most important show criteria: absolute symmetry of eyes in both shape and size.

BLACK MOOR

The Black Moor is a velvet-black Fantail with telescopic eyes. The jet-black coloration extends onto the abdominal region. It's a very impressive looking fish with many devotees. It must not be exposed to cold temperatures for prolonged periods of time. The Black Moor is a beautiful fish for the home aquarium.

CELESTIAL

This fish is actually a Telescope-eye with the eyes pointing upward (into the sky). The body is relatively long and slender, with a long, paired tail fin. The back is smooth and the dorsal fin is absent. The eyes must point straight upward and be of equal size. It's self-explanatory as to why such fishes find it easier to eat floating food at the tank's surface. Nonetheless, they're also capable of picking up food from the bottom. Celestials are rather sensitive to cold temperatures.

BUBBLE-EYE

The body form is similar to that of the Celestial, although there are more slender forms as well as one that is bred deliberately for a roundish body. The conspicuous characteristic of "bubble-eyes" is a bubble filled with a tear-like fluid, located underneath each eye. The eyes are pointed upward, and it is important that the bubbles are large and of equal size. It's also important that these fish are capable of swimming properly. Bubble-eyes, Telescopes, and Celestials can all be housed in the same aquarium. They are of similar temperament. The tank must be totally devoid of any sharp-edged objects which could injure the sensitive eye structures of these fish.

ORANDA

In body shape and finnage Orandas are similar to Veiltails, but they are conspicuous because of the "melon", a raspberry-like skin growth covering the entire head, except the eyes. These fish have well-developed "cheeks" which give them a unique facial expression. Oranda's occur in all goldfish colors, often in startling patterns. The Red-capped

An enormous rare black bubble-eye with tremendous eye sacs.

A red oranda with a nicely developed "hood" or "crown."

An award-winning calico pearlscale with fantastic scalation from head to tail.

Oranda is a silvery-white fish with a shiny red crown, that covers the upper part of the head like a cap. Generally, Orandas are hardy fish, but they do not like water temperatures that are very cold.

LIONHEAD

The Chinese Lionhead's name is derived from its strongly developed hood or crown. The body is compact and displays a gently arched back. The finnage is short with paired anal and caudal fins. The dorsal fin is absent. The back must be smooth and without any sign of growth.

The most common colors are orange and red-white. A beginner often mistakes the Lionhead for a Japanese Ranchu.

RANCHU

Fully-developed Lionheads and Ranchus placed side-by-side in the same aquarium are distinguishable even by the beginner as two separate breeds. The Ranchu is roundish with a more arched back, and a tail which is slightly bent upwards. The typical "crown" is even more developed. Beyond that, the finnage is also generally short, and colors are generally better developed. For the Japanese, the Ranchu is the crowning achievement of goldfish breeding. There are several Ranchu exhibitions each year with some of the blue-ribbon winners valued in excess of several thousands of dollars.

PEARLSCALE

The Pearlscale has the most rounded body shape of all goldfish breeds. Characteristic of this breed are the conspicuous pearl-like scales which give it its unmistakable appearance. It occurs in all goldfish colors; the most common ones are orange, white, white and red, and calico. The fins can be long or short. The anal and tail fins are paired. These fish should be fed sparingly since they are prone to having swim bladder problems associated with overfeeding. Pearlscales are to be handled very gently to avoid the loss of scales.

OTHER VARIETIES AND BREEDS

The fancy goldfish mentioned above are forms that are the most popular, but they're not the only ones in existence. Another one that should be mentioned is the Pompon, which has "bushy" out-growths of the nostril. These fishes are actually quite interesting, but high quality Pompons are hard to find. There are, of course, many cross-bred forms from among

A beautifully developed red and white lionhead with a smooth, slightly arched back.

all those listed above, but they're not important within the scope of this book.

QUALITY AND VALUE OF GOLDFISH

You can see from the descriptions given above how large the diversity is, and consequently how difficult it is for the beginning aquarist to assess the value of a particular fish which he or she wants to acquire. This is easy for common goldfish, which may be purchased at any pet shop, garden center, etc., for a dollar or two. The only thing to be concerned with is the appearance and overall health of the fishes chosen.

It can be more difficult for some of the fancy forms. If you are interested in top quality specimens, which can, depending upon the variety, cost up to a couple thousand dollars or more, you should look for a dealer who specializes in quality "show" goldfish varieties. It's also important to keep looking at all types of goldfish in order to get a "feel" for a quality fish.

This First-place red and white ryukin has all the necessary show criteria. It possesses excellent conformation, color, and activity.

Accommodation

In cartoons the goldfish is always portrayed swimming in a nice, round goldfish bowl. The poor goldfish! We must take that for what it really is ....a bad joke! If you place your goldfish in such a container without aeration, filtration, or frequent water changes, it will soon be dead. So, how do we properly house our goldfish?

To start out with we have to decide whether the fish are for an outdoor pond or for an indoor aquarium. These first considerations are important, because keeping goldfish outdoors in a garden pond immediately excludes temperature-sensitive forms. The previous chapter has shown us that goldfish are not only vastly different in appearance, but differ also in their particular requirements. Common goldfish, Comets and Shubunkins are really the only ones that can be left outdoors—in good conscience—right through the winter in a suitably built pond.

On the other hand, anyone willing to provide separate summer and winter accommodations for his goldfish opens the door for a larger number of varieties to choose from. But it must be remembered that keeping the same lot of fish on a seasonal basis, whether it be indoors or outdoors, can become quite involved. Finally, keeping goldfish only indoors makes virtually all known varieties accessible.

We would like to look at these three possibilities and provide you with certain selection criteria which may make your choice much easier.

Goldfish are not fussy when it comes to their aquarium accommodations. They may be housed in a variety of tanks.

Facing Page: A tremendous adult red and white oranda.

THE AQUARIUM

The obvious alternative to the goldfish bowl is the standard aquarium. If you want to fulfill your children's wish and set up a goldfish aquarium, please remember that even the hardiest goldfish, such as the common goldfish, has certain minimum requirements as far as tank space is concerned. Your best alternative is to purchase a standard, rectangular aquarium that allows the ratio of surface area to tank volume to be sufficiently large enough to facilitate adequate oxygen exchange.

•The tank volume must not be less than 10 gallons, and larger aquariums in the 30- to 50-gallon range are more appropriate. Fish don't care one way or the other as to whether you select an all-glass or acrylic tank. It's really only a matter of individual taste and the expense one can comfortably afford.

•A filter that has the capacity of turning over several gallons of water every hour is essential. There are several different types of filtration methods available. Both inside and outside filters work well. The modern outside power filters and canister filters are more attractive and can be conveniently hidden in back or below the aquarium.

•Lighting is also important. Both incandescent and fluorescent lighting are available. For water plants to grow properly, they require 10 to 12 hours of incandescent or natural light daily. Fluorescent lighting further enhances the color of the fishes and their surroundings. The tank must also have a cover (glass top or lid, including light fitting) so that fishes can't jump out. Aquarium covers may also be used to stop a cat from "going fishing." Slow-moving veiltails are easy prey!

•Goldfish are not tropical fish and therefore technically don't require an aquarium heater. However, it's important to remember that fluctuating room temperatures can have an adverse effect on aquarium water temperatures. Water temperatures that are not stabilized will increase the possibility of disease. An adjustable, thermostatically-controlled 50- to 100-Watt rod heater is sufficient in setting the desired temperature for 10 to 20 gallons of water. Don't forget the use of a thermometer to monitor the temperature.

•You will also need enough gravel to safely cover the bottom of the aquarium. It should be one and a half to two inches thick. Another recommended addition includes both live and fake plants. Both are available from an aquarium or pet shop. You are cautioned against harvesting plants from a local creek or pond or acquiring rocks or wood that are not aquarium safe. This could introduce pollutants,

parasites, and other toxic substances, all of which can put your entire goldfish stock in jeopardy. The dealer will advise you on what live plants are compatible with particular water temperatures. Goldfish have a preference for eating soft aquatic plants such as

must avoid all sharp, angular objects and narrow caves. Otherwise, the fish could injure themselves and the wounds could become infected. The tank must be set up before we go out and buy the fish. Once the tank is home the very first thing to

Delicate eye sacs of the bubble-eye are easily broken or damaged.

Elodea, which are always eagerly accepted. Other useful live plants for the aquarium are *Cryptocoryne, Vallesneria,* and *Sagittaria.*
•When selecting other items of tank decoration it is important to keep in mind what types of goldfish are going to be kept. For varieties with long, delicate fins and bubble-eyes, such as Celestials and Telescopes, we

check for is leaks. We fill the tank with water and let it stand for 24 hours. This test is especially important for tanks acquired second hand which may be more prone to leaking.
Once we are sure the tank holds water, it's taken to its ultimate location. In order to avoid (or compensate for) unnecessary structural stress, the tank is placed on top of a

styrofoam or felt mat. The gravel is then thoroughly washed and placed along the bottom of the tank, and some of the decorations (rocks, driftwood, etc.) are then added. The tank is then cautiously filled with lukewarm water (about 68° F). In order to neutralize any undesirable chemicals (e.g. chlorine), a quality water conditioner is added. A plate or saucer placed over the bottom of the tank will help prevent the gravel from unwanted stirring while the water is being poured. The tank is then filled about half way. Now the plants are added; this is done in such a way that the taller plants are placed toward the back of the tank. The foreground should remain free so that the fish can be seen. Planting must be done cautiously so that stems and roots of live plants are not damaged, and leaves are not broken off. The best method is to dig a hole into the gravel with a finger, while carefully placing the plant root into the hole, and filling it up again around the base of the plant.

The remaining tank space can now be filled almost to the surface, leaving just enough room for the filter and heater. If there are any problems related to the operation of tank equipment, the aquarium dealer should be able to solve any difficulties one may encounter.

Now that the aquarium has been properly set up, it's

Proper aquarium set-up requires patience, accuracy, and a knowledge of the equipment being used.

A well-planted aquarium provides a healthy environment for goldfish. Unfortunately, most goldfish enjoy the taste of soft water plants as well.

almost time to add the first fish. Prior to purchasing the first goldfish the filter, heater, and quality of the tank water should be checked. A reliable pH kit should also be purchased. The pH is the measure of acidity and alkalinity in the water. To check the pH, a measured amount of water is put into a test vial, and drops of indicator solution are added. The resulting color change is checked against a chart. A reading of 7.0 is considered neutral, and anything that exceeds that value is alkaline or goes below is acidic. Goldfish prefer the pH of their water to be neutral (7.0) or slightly alkaline. Then, finally,

you can add the fish. A 30-gallon tank can hold approximately 5 one-inch-long goldfish. This allows for appropriate growing space. A general rule is: Add one to one and a half inches of fish per-gallon of water. Resist the temptation to add more fish than that. Overcrowding the aquarium will result in an increase in waste products. This will over-burden the helpful bacteria which in essence keep the tank clean.

The filter removes any suspended particles, and so provides for clean and clear water. As mentioned above, water clarity can only be achieved in tanks that are not overstocked nor overfed.

The tank must be checked daily to see whether the fish are healthy and the equipment is working properly. In addition, a one third water change every two weeks is needed. Pre-conditioned tap water can then be added. Please make sure that the new water is of the same temperature as the water in the aquarium. The stress imposed upon goldfish exposed to dramatic temperature changes can lead to various diseases! If the tank water is allowed to evaporate, and the hobbyist fails to facilitate adequate water changes, ammonia will build to toxic levels, and the pH is certain to turn acidic.

.... INDOORS OR OUTSIDE?

If you have a garden, balcony, or roof terrace you may be able to keep goldfish outside during the summer. Of course, there are a few important points to be considered, so that this doesn't become a disaster.

Location Of An Outdoor Aquarium

Contrary to popular belief the aquarium must not be exposed to direct sunlight all day. Sunlight promotes algal growth which when allowed to grow excessively will often hamper the appearance of the aquarium. An ideal location is somewhere in the shade, or a semi-shaded spot

A nice pair of red and white ranchus.

where the tank gets sunlight only during the morning hours. The intense midday or afternoon sun can cause considerable damage. It is, of course, possible to create shade even in a sunny location by using tall grass, bushes, and trees, or by placing an awning over the tank.

The ideal location for an outdoor aquarium is close to a house, preferably adjacent to a terrace. This makes supervision easier and

about mosquitoes; they will not hatch in an outdoor fish tank because they are a welcome addition to the goldfish menu.

Setting Up An Outdoor Aquarium

An outdoor goldfish tank has essentially the same requirements as one that is kept indoors, only the dimensions are somewhat more generous. Aquariums kept outdoors can sometimes be exposed to considerable

A raised garden pond may deter outdoor predators from interfering with the well-being of your goldfish.

simplifies such maintenance tasks as feeding. Goldfish must be fed even during rainy periods when the garden soil is soaked and walking to and from the aquarium becomes difficult. Besides, a position close to the house makes it easy to monitor any predator's action (cats, birds etc.). Veiltail goldfish are not the fastest swimmers, making them potentially easy prey. Also, you want to enjoy your fish without having to walk long distances. Don't worry

temperature variations, which have a detrimental effect on the health of sensitive goldfish. Therefore, it is important to establish a certain minimum water volume requirement. The tank should contain at least 50 gallons and must have a minimum depth of 2 feet. The stocking rate must not exceed 1 goldfish per 10 gallons, unless the outdoor tank is equipped with a filter. If there are only a few underwater plants—or none at all—it is

The red cap oranda is one of the most popular goldfish varieties.

essential that a filter is installed.

The construction material for such a tank or vat is not that important. There are a large number of ready-made tanks or vats for use in gardens or on terraces. Containers that are partially or even completely in-ground have the advantage of not appearing so bulky. An additional advantage is that this type of installation is less prone to dramatic temperature fluctuations, since the surrounding substrate (e.g. garden soil) tends to act as an insulator. Such a vat can also be made out of cemented bricks or

from two-by-fours, and covered with a plastic pond liner. Whenever lumber is used, it's important to make sure that the wood is not chemically treated since fish are extremely sensitive to lumber preservatives or insecticides.

Caution must also be exercised with freshly cemented or concreted tanks and ponds. Cement contains caustic lime which must be properly leached-out before plants and fishes are placed into the tank. To insure the complete removal of any chemicals (from the cement), the tank is completely filled with water and left standing (without gravel, decorations, fishes, or plants), for about 1 to 2 weeks. It's then emptied and refilled twice for similar time periods. The inside of the tank is thoroughly scrubbed with a solution of 1 part vinegar and 10 parts water. Subsequently, it is rinsed out by directing a powerful stream of water over the entire inside surface area.

This procedure can be avoided if the inside of a cement or concrete tank is coated with a chemically inert paint, as is used for the inside of drinking water containers. Details should be discussed with a reputable paint supplier. Similarly, with all ready-made ponds as well as with pond foil, it is important that they conform to drinking water guidelines, and must not contain any potentially harmful chemicals. Harmful chemicals can be released into the water and subsequently poison the goldfish.

Outdoor fish tanks, in-ground vats, and pools are often without supervision for prolonged periods of time, and should be secured against any potential invaders. Cats and birds present a potential threat to goldfish kept outdoors. It's pointless to lead a prolonged battle against these animals, since they're only doing what comes

A goldfish tub provides the space for numerous underwater plants and a fertile substrate for them to root in.

naturally. Instead, it's far more prudent to secure the tank properly. Most land-based predators don't like to get their feet wet, and so it's usually sufficient to keep the water level below a steeply sloping wall, that doesn't provide for any foot-hold. If the tank is completely in-ground, the instructions

The Indoor Aquarium

Goldfish kept indoors only during the winter months are more practically housed in demountable or collapsible containers. The fish can also be kept in rain barrels or baby bathtubs. The only important thing is that the containers are totally free of poisonous substances. The size must of

Unlike the regular large koi that must be kept outdoors, the butterfly or veiltail koi is small enough for the home aquarium.

provided for garden ponds should be followed; this is to prevent small mammals from falling in, and, due to the steep side, can not get out of the water and subsequently drown.

Outdoor goldfish tanks are rarely ever suited for over-wintering the fish outside. They're usually too small and too shallow. Prior to the onset of dramatically declining winter temperatures, the fish are taken inside and kept in an aquarium equipped with proper filtration.

course conform to the space requirements of the fish to be accommodated. One alternative for keeping goldfish indoors temporarily (for the duration of winter), is to use a home-made, strong, wooden crate, lined with plastic pond liner. Care must be taken to avoid the puncturing of the liner by protruding screws and nails.

It's advisable to install a sufficiently large filter. The goldfish will have to be kept indoors from the beginning of November until the end of

A unique red and black telescope-eyed oranda with fringetail.

Facing Page: A beautifully landscaped fishpond offering a creative blend of rock structures and greenery.

April in a balanced climate. Beyond that, an indoor holding tank should be treated more or less like the aquarium (discussed above). This makes it easier to keep it clean. However, it's advisable to provide sufficient aeration so that the fishes will get enough oxygen. If the air flow is too strong, it can be regulated with a hose clamp attached to the air line (positioned somewhere between air pump [vibrator pump] and the air stone).

GARDEN POND

It has only been in recent years that the garden pond has gained popularity again. The use of plastic pond liners and the availability of ready-made ponds have made it possible to set up garden ponds on even the smallest property. These ponds are cheaper and easier to install than building a concrete pool from scratch. This book is not intended to provide detailed instruction on how to build a pond. Instead, it is intended as a guide for some of the points to be considered when setting up a goldfish pond.

A fishpond in which we intend to keep goldfish right through the winter has different prerequisites than a pond merely for water plants. Before we get to the details of location and equipment, we need to talk about the water. Some of our recommendations about setting up a pond will hopefully then make more sense to the beginning pondkeeper.

WATER

Water is always an acute topic among pondkeepers. Not only is its source important, but also how to keep it clean. Many aquarists or, more appropriately, pond keepers become frustrated because they are unable to maintain suitable water quality in their pond or fish tank. And yet, this is not difficult at all once we understand the principal biological interactions that take place not only in the aquarium but also in outdoor garden ponds.

Let us start with the origin of water. When we fill an aquarium or some other fish tank we simply use the municipal drinking water supply. This water is clean and the required volume is usually not very large. A pond requires a substantial amount of water and the pondkeeper may be inclined to use rainwater. However, we must be careful with such sources. Conveniently available water (rainwater, groundwater, springwater, riverwater, etc.), must not be used without proper water testing for possible contamination of poisonous pollutants. Even optically clean water can still contain harmful substances. The presence of chemical impurities can sometimes only be determined through laboratory tests. Therefore, water from natural water sources must be analyzed. Many impurities can be permanently neutralized by specially formulated water purifiers.

Take a water sample and have it analyzed by your local municipal water supply authority. This may be done by using a clean 1 liter bottle with screw top. The bottle is then submerged and filled with water. Screw the lid back on *under water*, because the remaining oxygen (in air or air bubbles) tends to affect the water quality parameters. Place the filled bottle in a styrofoam container which protects it against light and temperature variations. After that, the water sample must be taken to the water laboratory as quickly as possible. This entire procedure must be strictly adhered to so that the water analysis produces the correct values.

In an artificially created water world the biological equilibrium must first be established in order for all the functions in this microcosm to take place as required. In a newly set up garden pond it's easy to see how this equilibrium establishes itself step-by-step.

The pond is filled with plants and conditioned tap water. For a few days everything looks pleasant until the water suddenly becomes cloudy. Tiny, floating algae have established themselves. They feed on the minerals dissolved in the newly added water, and, depending upon the amount of sunlight, they develop

more or less rapidly. If the weather is warm and the pond gets sun all day long, you can expect extremely fast algal growth. In the meantime, water plants and the harmless floating algae have started to grow and so they too use nutrients. Eventually they become deprived of nutrients. They die off and sink to the bottom. Aerobic bacteria (i.e. bacteria which must have oxygen to survive), utilize the dead algae and converts them into carbon dioxide, nitrate, phosphate or sulfate. All these substances are valuable minerals and they act as fertilizers for the water plants. In order to perform these tasks, the bacteria need oxygen which in turn is produced by the water plants. The equilibrium has been restored. The water contains sufficient oxygen and the plants are growing well. Then, without warning, the water turns cloudy and all the fish are at the surface gasping for air and eventually get sick. What has happened?

Fish use oxygen and produce waste materials that are later converted to nutrients for the plants by aerobic bacteria. Up to this point the cycle is still intact. But goldfish also grow and reproduce. Consequently, when too many large fish occupy the pond and produce an increasing amount of metabolic waste products,

A pathway to the garden pool from the home makes feeding and other daily pool maintenance more convenient.

A red ranchu with excellent color. Sunlight during outdoor exposure helps enhance the color of goldfish.

that is, more than can be utilized by the plants, the following happens: because of an excessive amount of nutrients in the water, floating algae are starting to grow again. By clouding the water they (partially) inhibit light penetration to the underwater plants. They then start to vegetate and produce less and less oxygen, which the fish and aerobic bacteria must have to survive. Eventually, the oxygen supply at the bottom of the pond collapses and another type of bacteria takes over from the aerobic bacteria. These are anaerobic bacteria, i.e. those that don't need oxygen. But these (anaerobic) bacteria also produce methane, hydrogen sulfide, and ammonia. The pond's equilibrium collapses.

Once this happens many people give up and declare that keeping fish is too complicated and fill the pond with flowering plants. Ironically, it isn't difficult at all to initiate the necessary corrective measures. As an immediate "first aid", one third of the entire pond water is replaced with tap water. The new water provides adequate oxygen and a brief recovery for the fish. In addition, all feedings must stop. This doesn't cause any harm to the fish, but it does lower the organic load on the water system.

The next step is to quickly determine where the problem lies.

1st Problem: The pond is totally exposed to continuous sunlight. **Symptoms:** During sunny, warm periods there is rapid growth of the floating algae; the water turns cloudy and the fish suffer from lack of oxygen; the pH values are usually too high (above pH 8).

Solution: It is absolutely imperative that the pond get some shade. More underwater plants must be added, possibly a filter, and all feeding must stop until the pH has dropped to about 7.0 to

7.5. Water samples should not be taken from the surface, but a few inches below it. Because of the effect of solar radiation at the surface, the upper water layer usually shows different values than the water below. The pH measurements should be taken late in the afternoon, because at that time these values are at their highest.

2nd Problem: The pond contains too many fish.

Symptoms: Ammonia and nitrite values are too high, with a simultaneous strong algal growth causing the water to become cloudy. The bottom of the pond is starting to get covered with a layer of black, foul-smelling mud, the fish are starting to show signs of

Overgrown trees and brush around the pond provide shade and shelter during intense, hot summer days.

During the autumn months, decaying leaves and branches in the pond should be removed regularly.

disease, and they are often covered by external parasites.

Solution: Somewhat drastic measures are required. The pond must be drained, the mud removed, and, possibly, the entire pond disinfected. Since a pond with a large number of fish always brings problems, a filter should be installed. You may even consider enlarging the pond.

3rd Problem: There is something unexplainably wrong with the pond.

Symptoms: The fish don't look well, some may be dying; just when the plants seem to be vegetating they start to die off.

Solution: The exact cause may not be immediately obvious, and some investigative work may have to be done. It's not too uncommon to find a poisonous pollutant at play here; one that is given off either by the material used to line the pond or something that has been inadvertently introduced directly into the pond.

The most frequent causes are: Plastic liners produced from low-quality materials which release poisonous chemical substances, poorly cleaned concrete tanks, contaminated ground- or riverwater, or rainwater that has washed chemical substances off the roof, which has then leaked into the pond. Particularly dangerous are

A lemon oranda with excellent head growth.

common gardening chemicals which are still being used and which are invariably quite harmful to fishes. Lumber preservatives are often questionable, and the popular railroad sleepers are very toxic. These materials must never be used in and around a garden pond for goldfish.

In all of these cases the only solution is to exchange all of the polluted water with fresh tap water. For that purpose all fishes must be removed from the pond, so that it can be thoroughly cleaned. Fortunately, these sort of chemical poisoning cases are rather rare.

Anyone with a garden pond or aquarium should handle chemicals used in the house and garden very carefully. Many chemicals which are generally considered to be harmless can be quite dangerous to fishes. On a windy day insecticide spray can be carried over long distances, and so it may be more prudent to avoid using chemicals around the outside garden pond. As a general rule, it's advisable to test water quality at regular intervals, irrespective of what type of container the goldfish are being accommodated in.

LOCATION OF THE POND

As we have seen, location of the pond plays an important role in maintaining proper

The garden pond should be built in an area that's less prone to constant sunshine. Excessive sunlight can cause massive algae bloom.

water quality. It should be in a shaded or semi-shaded location so that algal growth is kept in check. Ponds that have already been built in locations that receive excessive sunlight don't have to be abandoned, but simply provided with shade. A permanent solution is planting bushes or trees that will provide shaded conditions for most of the day.

There are also rapidly growing giant grasses that not only provide shade fairly quickly, but also are very decorative (bamboo, small maple trees, etc.). Evergreen trees offer shade throughout the year and rhododendron bushes flower very attractively every spring. A pond can give a garden a totally new

landscaped appearance. Consultation with your local tree nursery should get you appropriate horticultural advice as to what can be planted around a pond. There are also a great number of suitable books around that can provide you with creative and imaginative ideas.

I had my first experience with a pond located in an overgrown courtyard of an old farm house. This courtyard was about 1000 square feet in size and surrounded by barns and a wall. It would get about 3 to 4 hours sun in the morning, and from then on was in the shade (even in mid-summer). The pond was planted with a water lily, *Elodea*, and many shallow-water plants. Pond depth was about 4 feet, the diameter about 10 feet. Initially, I was going to keep only native coldwater fishes until I introduced 5 minnows.

However, after 2 weeks of fruitless observation attempts, I got bored and added 4 common goldfish. Finally, I

would replace evaporated water, and once every week or two I would exchange some of the pond water for tap water. This all sounds relatively simple, and indeed it is as long as the provided recommendations are followed.

A truly magnificent pond display blending harmoniously into the outdoor setting.

could see fish in my pond. The minnows would flash brilliantly in the sun, but they remained hidden when the pond was in the shade. Although the pond didn't have a filter, there were never any problems with floating algae. The number of fishes relative to the pond size was fairly low and continuous direct sunshine was non-existent. During the summer months I

TYPE OF CONSTRUCTION AND SIZE OF POND

It is entirely a matter of individual taste and your available finances as to what style and materials are used for the construction of your goldfish pond. The least complicated way to build a pond is the use of a pond liner. This material is easily applied in virtually limitless shapes and forms. However, its important that the liner is of high quality (costs being the principal guide). Cheap liners can possibly contain poisonous chemicals which may be given off into the water and so have a harmful effect on fishes. These types of liners don't comply with drinking water guidelines. Pond liners must have a minimum thickness of 1 mm and be durable. Liners used correctly should line a sand bed of at least 2 inches thick. This prevents the liner from getting punctured by sharp, angular stones and rocks.

Although a number of suitable liners are now available in different sizes, colors, and thickness, you may also purchase them custom-made, so that they need not be cut to size.

Swimming pools that are no longer in use make ideal goldfish ponds. However, the water must be free of chlorine and other chemicals which could be harmful to the fishes. Should you consider building a large pond in your garden, you may want to use specially pre-formed clay bricks. This is not exactly cheap and is somewhat involved, but it is a very natural way to set up a garden pond. A number of manufacturers offer ready-made ponds that can also be assembled from individual sections.

We must also mention brick-cemented or concrete (poured) ponds. These provide considerable latitude in terms of shapes and forms, and are favored by those with a taste for Japanese landscaped water gardens. Since concrete and cement rendering release highly active caustic chemical material into the water (refer to Chapter on outside tanks), these ponds must be very thoroughly cleaned. It's recommended that all concrete ponds be coated on the inside with a special paint that's used for drinking water containers.

The size of the pond is primarily dependent upon the size of your property. It should have a volume of at least 600 gallons. The depth should be made deep enough so the fishes can survive the winter. If you live in an area where long, cold winters are common it is advisable to make the pond even deeper yet. It's important that all pond details and specifications are properly drawn up. You will save yourself a lot of trouble later if the correct dimensions are drawn up right from the start. Don't worry about the appearance of a large water surface area (the pond), which may initially look somewhat out-of-place in your garden. Within a couple of seasons the pond and surrounding landscape will have harmoniously blended into each other.

You may also want to give some thought to the different types of water plants used in the pond. Some have different

requirements in regard to water depth and surface area. If there are no aquarium shops, garden centers, or nurseries close by, most aquarium magazines provide addresses of specialized water

underwater plants. With the aid of sunlight, underwater plants convert nutrients taken up—by a complicated mechanism known as photosynthesis—into energy and in doing so give off excess

Water lilies are among the most desirable pond plants. With adequate lighting they grow and spread quickly on the pond surface.

plant nurseries. Only then you can decide which plants to use and at which particular depths to place them. It's wise to plan your overall planting program in advance.

PLANTS AND BOTTOM SUBSTRATE

One of the absolute necessities for a fish pond is

oxygen. Some of the durable underwater plants include hornwort (*Ceratophyllum*) and waterweed (*Elodea*). However, they must be planted in copious quantities if they are to fulfill their role as oxygen producers (about one quarter of the pond area). These plants can grow and spread quite rapidly, but since goldfish like to include some plant material in their diet any explosive growth of these plants will be inhibited. If these plants start to take over too much pond area, they can be thinned out with a small garden rake. You must be careful not to damage the pond liner. Before these plants are actually taken out of the pond they should be shaken vigorously so that any attached organisms drop back into the pond. They may be valuable food for goldfish.

Apart from that its essentially up to your individual taste and budget as to what water plants you want to have in your pond. The water lily is a plant with several large leaves which may eventually cover the entire pond surface. In doing so it limits the visibility of the fish and underwater plants. Upon

setting up the goldfish pond it's advisable to "plant" the underwater plants in gravel only, rather than clay. The plants will be able to extract enough nutrients directly from the water.

Water lilies should be planted in clay. The adding of fertilizer tablets is also helpful. The surface of the clay is covered with a layer of washed gravel so that only the water lily buds protrude. It's not necessary to cover the entire bottom area of the pond with gravel. In fact, this makes maintaining the pool that much more difficult. It won't be long before the wall of the pond will be quickly grown over with algae giving it a very natural look.

Placing swamp plants in an area of the pond that is away from its deeper parts is very attractive and at the same

This interesting group of water lilies would limit the visibility of fish and underwater plants if allowed to grow freely.

Canister filters are excellent for the removal of aquarium debris and thus provide clean, healthy water.

time quite useful. An arrangement such as this provides hiding places for amphibians and fish broods. It also gives protection against "four-footed" fishermen! Cats don't like to get their paws wet! It has been said that frogs and toads can't live in a goldfish pond, but that is incorrect. Frogs have spawned in my pond and both frogs and toads have actually spent the winter with the goldfish and koi (fancy Japanese carp).

Irrespective of what plants you select, never transplant them from natural ponds and streams. You may inadvertently dig up protected plants and be liable for a fine. In addition, there are other immediate dangers to selecting outdoor plants. Disease causing organisms and parasites can be introduced and cause harm to the fish.

FILTER

When you have a lot of large goldfish in your pond, maintaining the proper water quality can become a real problem. The most sensible solution to this problem is installing a pond filter. To be precise, you actually need two types of filters in order to clean the water properly. The most commonly used filtration is the mechanical retention (straining out) of coarse, solid particles such as fish fecal matter, floating algae, leftover food, leaves, and mud. Most filters use relatively fine media

such as foam rubber, synthetic nylon wool, or very fine quartz sand, which makes for a very fine-grained

surface area. Depending upon the weather conditions, size of the pond, and number of fishes in the pond, these types of filters will have to be cleaned very regularly; at least once a week and possibly as often as daily!

The swimming pool filter has several advantages, such as a backwash valve. This makes it possible to wash out the dirty filter medium and discard the backwash water. The disadvantage of such purely mechanical filtration lies in the fact that the water appears optically clean, but the dissolved metabolic waste products (nitrogenous substances) from the fishes are not removed. Nitrite and ammonia levels will rise and slowly poison the water. Although the water may be crystal clear never rely on appearance; instead examine and test it (ammonia, nitrite, nitrate, pH, dissolved oxygen) at regular intervals.

In terms of restoring pond and aquarium water back to its original pristine condition, the most effective filtration is by means of a biological filter. Such filters contain relatively coarse filter media, such as gravel, lava rock, or filter mats (the filter has a very porous surface which virtually never becomes clogged up). Within a period of several weeks or even months a 'biological

The outside power filter fits conveniently on the back of most aquariums.

lawn' of a variety of bacteria becomes established on the coarse filter medium elements (gravel, etc.). These bacteria "feed" on the harmful nitrogenous waste products given off by the fishes and convert them to less dangerous substances.

As we learned earlier the bacteria in a healthy pond will keep the water clean. They're the aerobic bacteria which must have oxygen in order to live. In other words, what takes place inside a biological filter can best be described as normal natural water purification, but this happens under controlled conditions, since we can easily provide additional aeration. This type of filter must operate continuously, so that the bacterial cultures, once they are established, do not dry out and die off. During the winter the density of the bacteria is of course seasonally low, so that during spring there can be a brief algal bloom, which soon disappears again. The advantage of this filtration method is that not only are the suspended particles removed, but also nitrogenous substances as well. Because of the presence of the bacteria, such a filter is self-cleaning provided it is sufficiently large.

Mr. Hilble and I have experimented extensively with different filters. In addition to goldfish, both of us also keep koi. Koi, because of their large size produce tremendous amounts of metabolic waste

A calico telescope butterfly tail. Notice the intense blue coloration, nice finnage, and round body.

placing a great strain on the filter. A complete filtration unit is one that first cleans the water mechanically and then biologically. There are numerous filters that fit this description that can be easily installed at any existing pond without requiring substantial modifications. Inside of these filters, water from the pond passes first through filter brushes, which retain large dirt particles, and then it flows over filter mats made of a coarse, loosely woven material, where bacterial cultures become established. However, before the water flows through filter mats it's enriched with oxygen, so that the bacteria have optimum environmental conditions. Most pond filtration systems are available in different sizes suitable for tanks and ponds of various shapes and volumes. Since the water flowing through these systems is first cleaned mechanically and then biologically they are extremely helpful. Maintenance and cleaning has been confined to a minimum, since only the mechanical pre-filter needs to be washed out occasionally. That is indeed a major work saver.

Buying Your Goldfish

Goldfish are available at any corner shop, or so it seems. Even department stores, supermarkets, and garden centers have goldfish for sale. This doesn't mean that goldfish from these sources are necessarily of inferior quality. If the fish look healthy and the shop's aquariums appear properly maintained, there is nothing to stop you from buying your fish there. Yet, for high quality fancy strains which, after all, may cost several hundreds of dollars it is advisable to go to a reputable specialist or breeder. Goldfish experts usually will guarantee that their fish originate from quality breeding stock.

Currently, the highest quality goldfish come from Japan and China.

HOW TO RECOGNIZE A HEALTHY FISH

In order to get a good comparison between different shops and the goldfish quality available in each, it is advisable to visit a number of dealers before deciding on a particular purchase. A reputable dealer has well-maintained tanks and the fish are active and look healthy. Take your time! Look closely at the tanks and the fish in them. The tanks must be clean and the water should be clear. The fish must be swimming around actively in a

This red oranda would be a wise choice if shopping for goldfish.

Facing Page: This lionhead is passing through a color change. All of the dark markings will eventually fade to orange,

A female calico bubble-eye of outstanding quality.

normal horizontal swimming position. They must not appear disoriented or injured. Do you see any external lesions on them? Are there any scales protruding or torn fins? Do some fish have "razor backs" or protruding eyes when they are not genuine Telescope-eyes? Are there even dead fish in some of the tanks? These are all signs of diseased fish or an entire diseased tank. We will discuss goldfish diseases in a separate chapter to help you easily recognize what may be wrong with a particular fish. A responsible dealer will not only get his stock from reputable breeders, but he will also see to it that the fishes in

his care are kept under optimum conditions.

TRANSPORTING AND INTRODUCING GOLDFISH INTO THEIR NEW HOME

A reputable dealer will see to it that your goldfish gets sufficient oxygen pumped into its plastic bag for the trip home. Goldfish can survive for several hours in plastic bags. Make sure that the fish are not exposed to temperature variations. During the summer months a hot car is particularly dangerous! Although goldfish can endure temperatures of up to 95°F, dramatic temperature changes over brief periods of time are invariably fatal for

Water conditioners help in removing any chlorine or harmful metals that may be present in your tap water.

these fishes. They are cold-blooded and will adapt their body temperature to that of the surrounding water, and are unable to cope with excessive changes. The potential injuries that can be incurred can range from gas embolism to serious swim bladder problems. This results in loss of equilibrium and eventual death of the affected fish. Therefore, newly purchased fish must never be poured directly from the plastic bag into the tank or pond. Instead, the closed plastic bag is floated on the water surface for at least 10 minutes so that the temperature of the water inside the bag gradually adjusts to that of the tank or pond. Only then is the bag cautiously opened and small amounts of tank or pond water permitted to flood into the bag. This process prevents the fish from going into traumatic shock.

Never place tap water directly into the new aquarium.

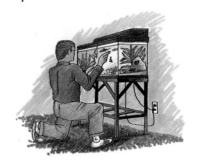

Care And Maintenance

Goldfish, especially the common variety, are relatively hardy and easy to keep. I'm saying this rather reluctantly about any fish since some people are then inclined to believe nothing could harm these fish or pose problems for them. Believing this could be a fatal mistake!

BASIC REQUIREMENTS

Many people still consider goldfish to be coldwater fish. This is not really correct. On the basis of its ancestry, the large group of carp-like fishes, which includes goldfish, belongs to the warm-water fishes. Goldfish may exist and survive at periods of low temperatures, but will only thrive and increase in size at median temperatures. To clarify this point: salmon and trout, which prefer cold mountain streams, are coldwater fishes. You can see that there is a significant difference.

TEMPERATURE

Temperature requirements of goldfish vary. The common goldfish, Comets, and Shubunkins can be kept outdoors throughout the changing seasons. All other varieties must be taken indoors during the winter since they can not tolerate extreme low temperatures. Goldfish exposed to very cold temperatures are more

Some aquarium thermometers may be placed inside or outside the tank for easy readability.

These garden plants are covered by solid ice.

susceptible to disease and the consequences can be fatal. Even goldfish that are kept inside the home must have their water temperature monitored closely. A standard aquarium heater may have to be used so that the goldfish will not die in an unheated room. Recommending an ideal temperature for all types of goldfish is difficult. As mentioned earlier, the most important aspect of keeping goldfish is not to allow the water temperature to drop or increase suddenly.

OVER-WINTERING IN A POND

The common goldfish has a broad temperature tolerance, but extremities of both low and high temperatures can only be tolerated for a short time. When you keep your goldfish outside during the winter, they will, during periods of declining temperatures, remain in the slightly warmer water at the bottom of the pond. They go into a semi-hibernation, whereby the physiological body functions are reduced to a minimum. In this state, the goldfish heart beats only 1 to 2 times per minute; on the other hand, during the summer, the heartbeat is 50 to 55 times per minute. But even in this state of semi-hibernation fishes must breath and so require oxygen. Therefore, the pond must not be permitted to freeze over for several consecutive days. It is essential for fouling gases (which develop in the mud at the bottom), to escape, and the pond water be able to take up oxygen again.

One bad habit common among pondkeepers is to plug the ice hole with straw in order to prevent it from freezing over. The straw invariably rots and so places a further burden on the water. At very low temperatures the straw is frozen over by the advancing ice. However, there are a few measures that can be taken, which will assure a relatively harmless over-wintering of the goldfish in a pond.

The most important prerequisite is a pond depth of at least 3 to 4 feet. This allows enough swimming room for the fish below the ice. If there is a sizable fish population it may be advisable to install an oxygen generator so that the oxygen content doesn't drop too low. An oxygen generator enriches the water with oxygen osmotically. Hydrogen peroxide inside the oxygen generator reacts slowly with water and so releases oxygen.

As a last resort the installation of a pond heater will most certainly prevent the water from freezing over. During long and cold winters a heater placed on the bottom of the pond will assure that the temperature doesn't drop below 32°F. Don't be afraid of excessive electricity costs. These heaters are adjustable,

and they operate only when the temperature drops below the freezing point, or below the set temperature, respectively. In addition, the filter return pipe should be located just below the pond surface, so that surface movement of the flowing water prevents the pond from freezing over.

One thing that must never be done is the chopping up of the ice cover! This creates sound waves that can be harmful to the fish. It causes them to move around and use up more oxygen. It's better to pour hot water on the ice causing a hole to form on the frozen pond cover. Of course, the most sensible thing is not to let the pond completely freeze over in the first place!

If you comply with all of these recommendations and you keep the pond clean from any other additional biological "load" on the water, such as decaying mud or other debris, the goldfish will over-winter without a problem. A

If the pond is deep enough, goldfish left outdoors can survive even the harshest winters.

feeding that consists of a nutritional diet is also helpful in successfully keeping them through the winter. If the winter turns out to be warmer than usual and the fish are getting active, it may become necessary to feed them since there will be little natural pond food available in the middle of the winter. But be careful that no uneaten food sinks to the bottom and then fouls the water.

Apart from that, a garden pond does not require much effort for successful maintenance. In autumn, during the time of falling leaves, it is important to make sure that not too many leaves end up on the bottom of the pond as they will quickly begin to decay. A net of any type is an effective retainer of fallen leaves. This is easier than trying to remove mud from the bottom of the pond. Yet, even with the best kept pond it may become necessary

An orange pom-pon telescope-eye.

to clean it thoroughly every 2 or 3 years. If you drag a small-meshed net over the bottom and it stirs up massive clouds of mud, it's a definite indication that it's time for a cleaning.

The mud from the bottom of the pond is black and smells foul. Such an occurrence signifies that not enough oxygen is available at the bottom of the pond, so that anaerobic bacteria have taken over the role of decomposing the organic materials. As we now know, these bacteria also produce methane, hydrogen sulfide, and ammonia. It often smells like rotten eggs! The easiest way to remove the mud is by means of a sufficiently large suction pump, which sucks up the mud and pushes it to the surface. Suitable pumps are available from most equipment rental outlets or they can be purchased from construction equipment suppliers.

Cleaning of this magnitude should be done in the fall, because the fish are in optimum condition and water plants have stopped growing. It's best to remove all fish and transfer them to a large tub or similar container. This is an opportune time to examine each fish for parasites or signs of disease and initiate the appropriate corrective action, if required. In the event there is a disease problem, the pond can also be treated while it's being cleaned out. For treatment details please refer to the Chapter on "Diseases."

Once the pond has been re-filled it is best to wait 2 or 3 days before the fish are returned. By the way, cleaning does NOT imply the use of household detergents and cleaners; this would be a sure way to kill all pond life. Instead, we use a garden hose and, if need be, a shovel and a brush. You must never use chemicals, except for products that are made specifically for fish.

OVER-WINTERING GOLDFISH INDOORS

Goldfish kept outdoors in a vat, tub, or small pool are certainly not in suitable accommodations for over-wintering. We have to take our fish inside once it starts to get cold outside. We catch the fish with a hand net and place them temporarily in a bucket filled with water from the tub. They're then taken to their new home which should have been filled with at least half the water from the outdoor tub or other container. It's important that there is no temperature difference between outside and inside water causing undue stress (temperature shock!). The fish should be examined for symptoms of disease, and if need be appropriately treated.

At this point, future care and maintenance of the goldfish is dependent upon the variety involved. The common goldfish, Comet, and Shubunkin are kept in tanks that are of suitable size for the

Bubble-eyes of this quality need large tank space, a nutritional diet, and optimum water conditions.

numbers and sizes of fish involved. One has to allocate at least one-and-a-half to two inches of fish per gallon. If you don't have a suitable tank or tub available in the size required, an easy alternative is to line a sturdy wooden crate with quality pond liner. This container can be placed in a cool, but frost-free room which has been slightly darkened so that the overall conditions resemble those in nature. For safety-sake it is advisable to install a filter along with adequate aeration, so that there is no lack of oxygen, especially when the fish prove to be more active than had been earlier anticipated.

The sensitive fancy goldfish (including Telescope-eyes, Ranchus, Celestials, etc.) must also be provided with a heater to maintain a stable water temperature in addition to filtration and aeration. Water temperatures kept in the high 60's to low 70's is ideal. These fancy varieties must also be fed small amounts at regular intervals. If the goldfish are thin and weakened by disease and parasites, they should be kept somewhat warmer and be given an appropriate amount of food to help them gain their strength.

GOING ON VACATION

What do we do with our fishes when we go on vacation or leave to visit relatives for the holidays? At the risk of sounding cruel .....preferably nothing! Most inexperienced aquarists that agree to look over your goldfish stock are certain to overfeed. The consequences of left-over, decaying food are far worse than having your fish fast for a few weeks. If your holiday or vacation is during the summer, the goldfish will find enough natural food in the pond, and so there is really no need for a caretaker, except for cleaning and monitoring the filter and other electrical equipment.

Goldfish tanks that are easily accessible to other animals must be covered with sturdy aquarium hoods or screens. It's also probably a good idea to have a neighbor occasionally check on the water level of the tank. During hot weather periods—without rain—considerable evaporation takes place, which can lead to problems.

If the fish must be fed you can always install an automatic food dispenser. However, if you don't stay away more than three weeks this is really not necessary. Proper filtration, lighting, and heating must also remain in operation, whereby the lighting can be controlled with an on and off switch. The heater can be turned down 4 or 5 degrees; which slows down the fishes' metabolism slightly. These adjustments should be made about 1 to 2 days before your departure to make sure everything is working as required. Filtration and aeration must operate continuously in helping prevent any respiratory difficulties. It's a good idea to have someone check every few days to make sure the equipment is working properly. One more recommendation: don't buy any new fish prior to departure for vacation. Should the new fish be diseased they could infect the entire pond population and you won't be around to notice it.

An automatic food dispenser can be easily set to the desired days and times for accurate feedings. This is advantageous to hobbyists who may be away from home for long intervals.

The Goldfish Diet

The best diet for fishes consists of food items occurring naturally in their surrounding environment. But, since your fishes are essentially in captivity it's up to the owner to provide a variable, balanced diet for them.

WHAT FOOD IS SUITABLE?

The goal of most goldfish fanciers is to feed their pets a diet which is as close as possible to one they are likely to find in the wild. Therefore, they breed worms and insects with much effort in terms of time and materials. This type

of intensive involvement isn't for everyone—and not really necessary either.

Goldfish foods are available in all types and varieties from shops everywhere. Even the local supermarket sells goldfish food. In fact, there are relatively few foods that goldfish will turn down. Your goldfish may eat different foods, but it may not always be the right kind of diet. There are some rather strange mixtures of goldfish and pond fish foods on the market. I have found insect larvae and beetles in newly opened cans of fish food, which had been

There are many brands of goldfish food on the retail market. An ideal goldfish diet includes not only dry food, but frozen and live foods as well.

sealed with an extra metal foil. Such contaminated foods are rare, and for the most part packaged foods are relatively safe and nutritional.

Goldfish will accept both flakes and pelleted food. The best food for larger goldfish are pellets, which are available in floating or sinking format. You have the choice among various grain sizes and nutritional quality. These

downward vision is limited. Although these fish can smell the food, its uptake should not be made unnecessarily difficult for them. A special treat for goldfish is the occasional live food. Live brine shrimp, bloodworms, daphnia, or tubifex are always accepted. It's important not to retrieve this food from contaminated waters. Frozen varieties of the above are also

Goldfish may be trained to take food from the hand.

pellets contain basic proteins, lysine, fat, roughage (fiber), carbohydrates, and are also fortified with vitamins and minerals. The Japanese distribute an excellent food which contains shrimp meat and carotinagenous algae which enhances coloration. It is very expensive, but an ideal food especially for the fancy goldfish varieties such as Red-Capped Orandas. Celestials and Bubble-Eyes prefer floating food, since their

readily available and an excellent source of food.

For those interested in culturing their own live food it isn't very difficult. A simple rain-barrel can become a hatchery for water fleas, mosquito larvae, and other small aquatic insects. How is this accomplished? It is very simple. Just fill a rain-barrel or similar-sized container with water; let it stand for a while occasionally adding some baker's yeast (from a drug

Frozen foods are nutritional additions to the goldfish diet.

store). A number of aquatic life forms will develop all on their own; insects deposit their eggs in the water and the larval forms will suddenly appear in abundance. This same method and procedure should also work on a "balcony", although I have not yet tried it. This way you always have fresh, inexpensive live food for your goldfish, which can also be used as a protein supplement.

One basic rule applies to all live fish foods: they must never have been in contact with poisonous chemicals! Fishes are extremely sensitive to insecticides, herbicides, and chemicals in general. This is of particular importance when feeding earthworms or other insects from your garden or other areas outside your control and supervision. Ideally, your garden should not be sprayed at all. This allows for all the insects collected to be fed directly to the fish.

Most goldfish breeders and hobbyists prefer to make homemade foods. Supplying the goldfish with a diet of spinach, peas, and thinly sliced green beans is ideal in satisfying their preference for greens. Vegetation in their diet is also helpful in achieving maximum growth and color and should be given as frequently as possible.

HOW MUCH TO FEED

It is difficult to state categorically how much to feed each fish. There are too many factors involved in determining the precise food requirements for a particular goldfish. This is influenced by the size of the individual fish, the environment it lives in, the temperature, season, etc. Initially you must take your time when feeding your fish. Floating pellets are easy to feed since you can closely monitor how much has been taken in one feeding. To start out, toss a few grains to each

fish to attract them. Once the fish have accepted the food, you continue in the same fashion until you notice that the fish are clearly less eager to feed. They are then full! This can happen after 2 to 3 pellets or after many more; it depends on the size of the fish and the ambient water temperature. Feed only for 1 minute and no longer! A goldfish can't feed indefinitely and overfeeding is one of the major causes of failure in the hobby. If after 60 seconds there is food floating, or settled on the bottom of the aquarium, you have undoubtedly overfed. The largest demand comes during the summer from fishes kept outdoors; the appetite of aquarium-kept fishes is greater even throughout the year since there are little or no seasonal changes in water temperature.

FEEDING TIMES AND LOCATION

It makes sense in having your fish adjust to a specific feeding site. This makes it easier to control the amount of food given to each fish, rather than distributing the pellets all over the pond or pool. Better yet, it facilitates closer supervision of all the fish especially in regard to disease control. If one of the fish doesn't come over to get food and keeps to itself, it may be the first indication of a problem. Once the fish have adjusted to a particular feeding site they will come over as soon as you approach the pond or tank. This is particularly obvious at a pond where goldfish have a tendency to hide among underwater plants or below the floating leaves of water lilies. When you approach the feeding site there is suddenly

A feeding cone filled with bloodworms or tubifex worms is a fun and interesting way to feed your fish.

A beautiful black telescope.

life, and a school of fish appear out of nowhere to feed eagerly. Goldfish always act like they have been starved. Don't be fooled or misled into overfeeding them. Once you have established the appropriate amount of food to feed, spread it out over 2 to 3 feedings a day.

During the summer it is best to feed in the morning, and again in the late afternoon. If your schedule only allows enough time for one feeding a day make sure that you take your time. Only feed what the goldfish are willing to accept. Uneaten food will decay quickly and may very well pollute the entire tank or pond.

Behavior

GOLDFISH AND THE OTHER FISHES

Goldfish are peaceful animals which are quite compatible with other fishes. However, there are a few reservations in respect to Veiltail Goldfish and the Bubble-eye and Telescope-eye breeds. Because of their slow movements and delicate external features, they can easily be injured and are at a disadvantage when searching for food. Therefore, these goldfish varieties should be kept together with fish of similar temperament. Adding new goldfish to an already existing (aquarium or pond) population usually doesn't present any problems. In ponds, or very large tanks, they usually band together in loose schools, but they also like to hide individually among underwater plants and under floating leaves of water lilies. Goldfish don't practice brood care and won't recognize their young. They will

pursue them until the fry are about 3 to 4 cm long.

Goldfish are friendly creatures that can become hand-tame provided you spend a lot of time with them. If you toss a few grains of food to the fish every time you approach the pond or tank, they'll soon recognize you and swim over when you are at the pond. But still, make sure you are not overfeeding your fish.

For me personally there are two groups of goldfish and also two different methods to look after them. I adore Veiltails in all their different varieties. I enjoy watching them display their glorious finnage in an aquarium. I like

Slow-moving goldfish are at a disadvantage when searching for food.

Ranchus and Orandas with their unique head growths and fascinating facial expressions. I also admire the Black Moor which makes a spectacular addition to any aquarium.

The goldfish pond opens another world to me. It's a sharing in nature. A water world of both harmony and cruelty at the same time. This to me is the realm of the more robust common goldfish, Comets, and Shubunkins. Here I can experience my goldfish within a setting of changing seasons, their active courtship, their first tiny, barely visible, young fry which seem to be nothing more than a pair of eyes. How many of these baby fish will make it through to the fall?

BREEDING GOLDFISH

Although goldfish may be bred in the home aquarium, the easiest way to breed goldfish is in a pond. The pond provides the fishes with a natural environment, helping to stimulate them into spawning. Sexual maturity is reached at the end of the second year. Breeding commences in early summer when the water is getting warmer. A pair that's preparing to spawn are easy to distinguish. The females become more plump and their enlarged abdomens are clearly visible when viewed from above. The males develop tiny, white, pin-sized spots known as tubercles on their gill plates and pectoral fins.

To an inexperienced goldfish hobbyist the courtship and breeding behavior of these fish may be quite frightening. The otherwise normally peaceful fish begin chasing each other in what appears to be an aggressive manner, as if they were fighting. The truth is that the females, ready to spawn, are usually pursued and courted by several males wanting to mate with them. During spawning the males become very persistent, and it appears as if the females are virtually pushed out of the water. Hornwort and other soft aquatic plants are used as appropriate nesting sites, since they afford the greatest protection to the eggs and young.

Goldfish can also spawn in the aquarium, but it's often difficult to raise the brood under such confined conditions. This is a labor-intensive and difficult procedure which should be left to the breeder or experienced aquarist. If we want to raise goldfish in an aquarium it is safer to buy juveniles (1 to 2 inches), which are often available at reasonable prices. From among those hatched only very few make it through to adulthood.

ANATOMY

In this chapter we are going to acquaint you with details about the anatomy of goldfish. It's important to know the body parts and organs, so

A pair of goldfish begin the spawning sequence.

The eager male pursues the female.

Spawning is usually accompanied by much splashing and horseplay.

that in a discussion on diseases we would know what is being talked about. The typical fish body is divided into the head region (tip of snout to end of gill cover), the rump (end of gill cover to anal opening), and the tail.

The most important locomotory organ is the tail. When we observe different goldfish varieties for a while we notice how distinctly the various tail fin shapes define characteristic swimming motions. Those forms with a single tail fin display the most common form of fish locomotion. These fish either glide along with slight undulating motions of the tail, or dart through the water with rapid, whip-like lashes. Goldfish varieties with a double tail fin, be it short or long, "fan" with the entire posterior end of the body and the tail. This gives these fish the characteristic sequence of movements common to Veiltail goldfish. These fish are distinctly slower than those with a single tail fin, because not only are their tail fins being used, but also part of their body. The dorsal fin, pectoral fins, pelvic fins, and anal fin serve mainly as stabilizers and to change direction. The goldfish can swim in reverse with paddle-

Facing Page: White spots are present on the gill cover of this black moor, indicating his readiness for spawning.

A truly odd celestial with a close-up of its gold-encased eyes.

A great view of the head growth of this white lionhead. The size and shape of the head depends on genetics, nutrition, and water quality.

like movements of the pectoral fins.

The fins consist of skin supported by skeletal (fin) rays. Fins that have been damaged or torn will generally grow back provided they haven't been chewed that severely. How the fish holds its fins tells us a lot about the health of the fish. Fins folded tightly against the body is a good indicator that not all is well.

An important organ in goldfish is the mucous envelope. A healthy fish feels slippery to the touch. When a fish is handled or caught it's important not to damage the mucous envelope. This serves to protect the fish's body against an invasion by bacteria or fungi. Never hold a fish with dry hands or even with a dry rag! The mucous envelope is renewed from the skin of the fish. Only a fish on a proper diet can develop a sufficiently strong mucous envelope.

The scales act primarily as protection against major injuries, and are embedded in pockets made of connective tissue. They grow at the same rate as the fish, and in doing so they lay down growth rings on each scale, very similar to those indicating growth and age in trees. Scales that have been lost generally are replaced, unless the site becomes infected. There is, however, one difference with Pearl-Scale Goldfish: when these fish lose a scale, the replacement scale is not pearl-like but flat instead.

Respiration of fishes is accomplished through the gills. When a fish breathes it takes water in through the open mouth. It's passed over the gills and out again through the opercular opening. During this process there is a gaseous exchange, whereby oxygen is replaced with carbon dioxide. This same gaseous exchange also occurs in the human lung. If the fish lives in clean water and is healthy, the gills are blood-red. They are made up of very thin, lamellae-like plates which are located on cartilaginous gill arches. Rapid and severe raising and lowering of the gill cover with a simultaneous opening of the mouth, indicates the fish is suffering from a lack of oxygen.

Goldfish do not have any real teeth, only grinding plates located deep in the back of the mouth. These grinding plates are referred to as pharyngeal teeth. The goldfish macerate their food before it enters the digestive tract. These plates are so powerful that even hard cereal can be ground up. Food is further broken down into a liquid state by various enzymes located in the stomach.

In order to be able to adjust its weight in response to water pressure, the goldfish has a swim bladder. With the aid of this hollow, gas-filled organ the fish can determine whether it wants to sink, rise, or remain at a particular level. The swim bladder consists of two chambers and is

A pom-pon oranda with an out-turned operculum which is the bending of the gill cover. This is usually a flaw in genetics.

A trio of bright red orandas with large head growths.

has to take a very close look in order to see the thin line of pores that extends horizontally along the midline of the body. Fishes use this organ to perceive the slightest of vibrations; for instance, it can sense when you approach the aquarium or pond. Now you can understand how terrifying it must be for goldfish if you pound a hole into the ice surface of a pond.

Goldfish can also see very well and distinguish between colors. Like all fishes, goldfish have no eyelids. Their nostrils are located on both sides of the head just in front of the eyes. They each lead to an internal pit containing many skin folds. These are the olfactory pits and are used in smelling. Goldfish can smell as well as a dog can. They recognize food, siblings, and also enemies with their sense of smell. Goldfish are often observed picking up aquarium debris from the bottom of the tank and then spitting it out again. Sometimes a fish picks up something repeatedly, as if it was not sure whether it liked the taste or not. With the aid of taste buds located inside the mouth, fishes can actually taste and therefore determine whether something edible or inedible has been picked up. Fish food is

connected to the intestine. When a young goldfish hatches from an egg it is not yet capable of swimming, and so it attaches itself to water plants. After three or four days the young fish attempts to reach the water surface in order to take in some air to fill its swim bladder. If the young fish does not succeed it will die within a few days.

Goldfish become sexually mature at the end of the second year depending upon environmental conditions. The sexual reproductive organ of male goldfish is called the testes which produces the "milt" or sperm; female sexual organs are known as ovaries. Under normal conditions goldfish can reach an age of 10 to 20 years. In some rare instances goldfish have been known to live to the ripe old age of 40!

SENSORY ORGANS

One of the most important—yet for us barely visible—sensory organs is the lateral line organ. One really enriched with flavorings of fish oils for greater taste appeal.

Goldfish possess a well-developed inner ear, the labyrinth. It serves to perceive sound waves, and at the same time it maintains the fish's equilibrium. Fishes use it to

skin appears as "blue". Goldfish look brightest in a dark aquarium, since the pigments contract against the dark background.

SCALES

The scales, in addition to colors, define the external

Top view of a calico pearlscale with nice pearling.

orient themselves as to their actual position in the water, and to control turns and rolls. Sound waves are picked up via the skin and musculature by the swim bladder. From there they are passed on to the inner ear.

COLORS

The basic colors of goldfish are black, red-orange, and yellow. All other colors are combinations of the three base colors. The color pigments are located inside the skin as well as embedded in the scales. Pigments are located at different depths and will overlap, thereby creating a variety of colors. "Black" eminating from deep in the

appearance of goldfish. Most commonly represented are scales with a metallic sheen caused by deposits of guanine crystals inside. Transparent scales give fishes more of a "naked" appearance, as if the fishes didn't have any scales at all. The third type is a mother-of-pearl-like scale which is virtually opaque. These three types of scales may be seen separately or mixed together. One peculiarity is the "Pearl Scale." It has scales that have become thickened to such a degree that they resemble a half-pearl. However, if the Pearl Scale loses a scale it will only be replaced with a normal, flat scale.

A fabulous black male broadtail moor.

FINS

The fins are a characteristic peculiarity of Veiltail Goldfish. Based on the fins alone, there are so many variations that one is inclined to believe that we are dealing with different fish. It starts with the common goldfish and the Shubunkin, which have short, single tail fins. Similarly, Comets (with long and narrow fins) and Bristol Shubunkins (long- and broad fins) both have a single, forked tail.

The double-tailed goldfish varieties display a large number of fin shapes, from short to long and from shallowly to deeply forked. Ranchus, Lionheads, Bubble-Eyes, and Celestials are commonly being bred without a dorsal fin.

BODY SHAPE

The single-tailed varieties are relatively slender and fast swimmers. The double-tailed goldfish varieties have bodies that are more compact to roundish. There are, of course, standards which define the ideal shape of particular goldfish varieties, but such breeding ideals of absolute perfection are rarely to be found and therefore very expensive when they do occur.

EYE SHAPES

The goldfish has large eyes, which in most varieties are located on the sides of the head. But there are also breeds with telescopic eyes where the eyes are more or less protruding. The eyes of the Celestials and Bubble-eyes are directed upward; the

Above: This calico oranda has good head growth and nice black streaks in the fins.

Left: A rare pom-pon celestial.

latter also has blister-like sacs underneath the eyes which are filled with a tear-like fluid.

HEAD SHAPE

The head shape of a goldfish is generally more or less narrowly triangular. Orandas, Lionheads, and Ranchus carry a raspberry-like skin growth on the head. This gives them the appearance of a small, chubby-cheeked person.

ENEMIES

Most of the dangers for goldfish lurk outside, when they are kept in garden ponds or some other outdoor tank. While some of these dangers may be exaggerated, once we know who is after the lives of our outdoor friends we can then take adequate precautions and things aren't nearly as bad as originally thought.

Most threatened, of course, are young (newly hatched) goldfish. They fall victim to various predators including aquatic insects and also their own parents! But since goldfish produce a large number of progeny, we usually don't even notice when a few are missing. Besides, if there was no natural culling the pond would soon be terribly overcrowded. The quickest and healthiest fish hide among the green plants, so that natural selection virtually assures the development of healthy, future generations. Appropriate protective measures have to be instituted so that the goldfish brood is not lost.

Ectoparasites, which include leeches, fish lice, anchor worm, etc., can have severe effects among young goldfish since they're not yet as resistant as adult fish. It's important to make sure ponds and aquariums are free of parasites, and, if need be, appropriate eradication measures are taken.

Several birds, such as crows, magpies, and even

A Chinese lionhead with excellent head growth. The head covering is remarkably thicker when compared to the rest of the body.

A red and white telescope-eye butterfly tail. Notice how the tail is held parallel to the ground, appearing like butterfly wings from above.

ducks, like to go fishing. In a frequently used garden with lots of peripheral activities, bird predators should be an exception, unless we have introduced the birds there ourselves. On rarely visited weekend properties the risk is larger and considerable damage among fish populations in a small pond are quite possible. There is also a possibility that cats may go on fish hunts. Unfortunately, some cats like to catch fish, but, fortunately, not too many are successful at it. Some cats can peacefully co-exist with a fish pond in the garden without ever getting an idea to go fishing there themselves. I have three cats. My three month old female cat fell into the pond by mistake and ran across the water lily leaves so fast that only its feet got wet. The cat's back was bone dry. While this cat keenly watches the fish it makes no attempt to catch any of them. On the other hand, my male cat, to whom I once gave a dead goldfish that had not made it through the winter, keeps trying to catch goldfish. He's been successful three times. Since I don't have the time to constantly watch the cats, I've made the pond "cat-proof", and now there is peace! As you have seen from the example with the little female cat, cats don't like to get their feet wet. This aversion to water can be used quite effectively.

As mentioned before, for an outdoor vat or similar tank, a considerable drop from the upper edge down to the water level is usually adequate to deter cats. We have to use a different method for a pond, which is also commonly visited by other harmless animals that could fall into

Facing Page: Top: A juvenile red oranda. **Bottom:** Nicely colored calico fantail.

A brilliantly colored black oranda with superb conformation.

the water and drown. An ideal cat-proofing method is to set up a shallow water area along the pond's periphery, that is separated from deeper water by a stone barrier. This does permit the fish brood into the shallow water, but these small fishes are usually of no interest to cats. The rocks must be about 1 cm below the surface, which may also provide hiding and breeding grounds for frogs and toads. If the area around the pond slope is steeper, the water level must be at least a foot below ground level so that cats can't reach the water with their paws.

There is, of course, one important point that needs to be emphasized again: expensive Veiltail Goldfish, which aren't the fastest swimmers, shouldn't be left to themselves in a garden pond or in some other easily accessible container.

With all the precautions mentioned against protecting against the threat of animal predators, we shouldn't forget our fellow men as sources of aggravation when it comes to a garden pond. If you are living on a busy street, you may want to do without a goldfish pond in your front yard. I've often been annoyed with the poor habits of our neighbors in their constant dumping of garbage into the front yards of other people. The real danger comes from cigarette butts. The highly poisonous nicotine can have fatal consequences in the garden pond.

Diseases

The appearance of a diseased fish is usually an indication of inadequate care and maintenance. A fish kept under optimum conditions rarely gets sick. The main problem in keeping fish healthy is undoubtedly the element in which they live—the water. Clean water is as important to fishes as unpolluted air is to us. We all know, especially from the topical problems with environment and air pollution, how vitally important clean air is. Asthmatics and many people with allergies have experienced these ill-effects first hand. With that in mind, what is being experienced by a formerly healthy fish that swims, day after day, in its own excrements? Oxygen becomes scarce, its gills start to disintegrate, and the fish starts to look skinny or undernourished despite how well it's fed. At that stage, of course, the fish becomes very susceptible to fungal, bacterial, and viral infections, along with parasitic invasions, and is then visibly sick.

It's very difficult for us to put ourselves into the fish's position. There is no way of knowing how well it feels or whether or not it's in any pain. Unfortunately, a fish is not in a position to tell us or show us what is wrong. But with adequate information on hand and the knowledge and understanding of the biological processes that take

A calico telescope butterfly with a broken dorsal.

place in a pond or aquarium, it is easy for us to provide a healthy environment for our goldfish. After all, the best disease prevention is providing optimum care and maintenance and the know-how to do so.

PARASITES AND FUNGI

Ectoparasites occur in an outdoor location principally during the summer season. Like most organisms, they breed in spring and then mature during the summer. The fishes they attack usually behave quite conspicuously: they rub the affected body segment over rocks, along branches and other objects. That, by itself, is not proof of a parasitic infection. Take a close look at the fish and look for any rubbing that occurs frequently and at short intervals. Observe each fish intensely, even the ones that have behaved inconspicuously so far, because parasites sometimes change their host.

Goldfish kept in an indoor aquarium usually have fewer parasite problems, except when plants and sand used in the tank have come from outdoors. That is one sure way to introduce disease that will often go unnoticed. In some instances it may be days or weeks later before there is any indication of disease. Besides, it's best to keep outdoor plants in their natural surroundings since aquatic habitats are already encountering enormous pressures.

This oranda has an ulceration on its body, possibly the result of poor environmental conditions.

A calico fantail that is the unfortunate victim of excessive ammonia build-up. The streaks of blood are clearly visible through the fins.

Now a word about parasite medications. These substances are usually poisonous and highly potent since their intentions are to kill live organisms. As we know from insecticides, these substances also destroy organisms that we wish to keep alive. It's extremely important to follow the dosage recommendations explicitly. An overdose could cost you your entire fish stock. Calculating correct medication dosages is sometimes tricky in a large pond and isn't as easy as the standard indoor aquarium. Here's a helpful tip: when filling the pond take the appropriate readings of your water meter! If your fish have been severely affected by parasites, it may be advisable to take them indoors for the winter. The goldfish may have become too weak to survive outdoors during adverse winter conditions. If the fish has lesions, swellings, or even open wounds, it's better to keep them inside and to treat them with the appropriate medication. The empty pool should also be treated with the full dose, as per direction. The fish are then kept at about 68°F and given adequate feedings ensuring proper recovery. Toward the end of April or so (depending on the weather) the fish are taken outside again and released into the clean, parasite-free pond. The temperature of the indoor holding tank must not be drastically lower than the holding tank.

Parasites, fungi, and bacteria also live in clean water. They only become a danger if the fish are weakened by unsuitable environmental conditions, and their immune system is no longer capable of mustering an adequate physiological defense. A strong, healthy fish, which has been affected, for instance, by leeches will rub along rocks and stones in order to free themselves from parasites. These parasites cause small, open wounds which normally heal quite well; but bacteria and fungi can enter the fish's body via these open wounds and the fish can become sick. If the condition of the fish is poor to begin with, its body has no defense against these additional disease carriers.

It's now probably better understood as to why we must keep aquarium water and the fish's living quarters absolutely clean. After all the necessary steps for caring for your goldfish have been taken, it can safely be said that you've done your best in keeping your goldfish free of any possible health hazards. Monitor your fish closely at all times. Early detection of disease offers the best opportunity for successfully conquering sudden ailments.

Goldfish that spend a great deal of time at the aquarium bottom may be giving a clear indication that all is not well.

This especially goes for fishes that are being kept outdoors, whereby both fish and container (pond, aquarium) must be thoroughly inspected, so that any possible parasite or other health problems can be taken care of well before the onset of winter. During the winter the fish are slow and can't fend off these pests. The cold winter months brings on a prolonged fasting period of the fish which makes them weak and more susceptible to health problems.

ANCHOR WORM (*LERNAEA CYPRINACEA*)

This parasite grows to a length of about 15 mm. It drills into the skin of the fish, and looks as if two thin wires inside a colorless shell had been stuck into the skin. The point of penetration is usually also severely infected. The parasite has become "anchored" inside the muscles of its host where it destroys tissue and sucks blood.

Treatment

The parasite is relatively easy to remove from the fish by using a pair of forceps. In order to assure total treatment and success, the tank or pond must also be treated with appropriate medications. A brush that is dipped in potassium permanganate and placed on the parasite is a useful method in treating them.

LEECHES

Most leeches are introduced into the home aquarium through plants and other material collected from the wild. Their large size makes them easy to detect even for the inexperienced hobbyist.

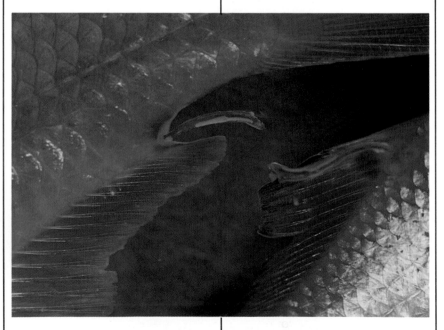

Anchor worms on the skin of goldfish.

The body is worm-like with a large sucking disc at each end. The leech finds optimum conditions in heavily overgrown, muddy waters without current. The carp leech can remain motionless for days, attached by its posterior suction cups to a plant leaf, erect, and pointing

Treatment

Aquarium treatment includes bathing the infected fish in a salt bath for 15 minutes. The leech can then be removed with forceps.

In the outdoor pond, 1 g Masoten to 50 gallons of water has proven to be an affective means of treatment.

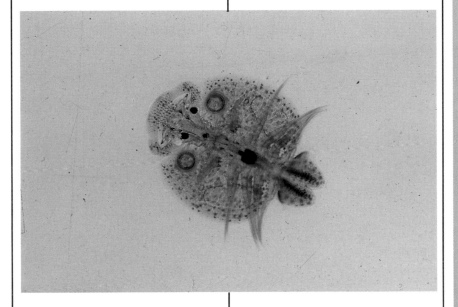

Fish lice (*Argulus foliaceus*) are parasites that occasionally attach themselves to goldfish.

into the open water until a fish swims by. The leech finds the fish with far-extended sweeping motions. As soon as it finds a victim it will let go of the plant leaf and penetrate the skin of the fish with its sucking mouth. Mating occurs on the host. The egg cocoons are subsequently deposited on rocks and plants. Although a few leeches can't kill a healthy fish, the point of penetration can become infected. However, massive infestations can lead to fish mortality.

FISH LOUSE (*ARGULUS FOLIACEUS*)

This parasite grows to a length of up to 6 mm. Its body is flattened and circular. It's essentially transparent and difficult to see on a fish host. However, the large, black eyes are often noticeable. The fish louse swims about until it encounters a host; usually this is a fish, but it may also be a tadpole. The parasite attaches itself and penetrates the host's skin with its stiletto-like feeding organ, which sucks out blood and tissue fluid. Commonly, inflammation and swelling develops around the puncture wound. The fish louse can be introduced through the feeding of daphnia, so special care should be taken when preparing this food.

Treatment

1 g Masoten in 80 gallons of water. Treatment is to be repeated in 5 to 6 weeks to kill any larvae that have hatched in the meantime. Allowing the pond or aquarium to dry out for 7 days may also kill both eggs and adults.

VELVET DISEASE

This disease can be caused by a number of organisms; they can be several species of unicellular dinoflagellated organisms, such as *Costia*, *Chilodonella*, or *Trichodina*. These parasites occur primarily just before the onset of winter or after a prolonged, cold winter. The disease may also appear when fishes haven't been kept properly. It

manifests itself by the appearance of a bluish-white veil-like layer over the entire body of the host. Some of the skin may actually flake off from the body. The disease tends to spread very rapidly under overcrowded conditions and is usually fatal for juvenile fish.

Treatment

The aquarium trade offers a number of effective over-the-counter remedies. If, contrary to expectation, none of them produce appropriate results, then you may have to dip your fish. This is often achieved through the use of a formalin solution (1 ml formalin [28%] dissolved in 5 liters of water); the fish must remain in this bath for 30 minutes. Otherwise, prepare an ordinary salt solution of 15 gm NaCl [household salt] dissolved in 1 liter of water. The fish must remain in the solution for an hour. Don't alter the dosage recommendations. Another effective method is the use of copper sulfate. Appropriate dosages are available on each manufacturer's package.

WHITE SPOT DISEASE (ICH)

This disease is caused by the ciliated parasite Ichthyophthirius. It can be recognized by the presence of tiny white nodules on the skin and fins of the fish. The fish actually look as if they've

been sprinkled with salt. Parasite development is encouraged through bad water quality, overcrowding, or frequent additions of make-up water straight from the tap.

parasites, such as tapeworms, flukes, and roundworms are difficult for the beginning aquarist to detect. Therefore, we won't go into great detail here. Fishes that are greatly emaciated or extremely fat can

A goldfish that has damaged its mucus envelope, possibly the result of scraping itself on a sharp-edged aquarium object.

Treatment
There are several types of effective commercial treatments for ich available from local pet shops and aquarium dealers. One of the old methods of treating ich, that is still used and effective is the use of a dye, either malachite green or methylene blue. Regardless of the type of medication used, the importance of following the manufacturer's directions can't be emphasized enough.

INTERNAL PARASITES
Diseases caused by internal

be indicative of a massive infestation of internal parasites. This can also be caused by other diseases so its best to seek advice from an expert (aquarium shop owner or fish specialist).

FUNGUS (*SAPROLEGNIA*)
The healthy mucus envelope of a goldfish acts like a protective shield against *Saprolegnia* spores. Mucous envelopes that become damaged offers a ideal site for a fungal invasion. A fish can cause damage to its own mucous envelope by scraping

along a sharp-edged stone. Wounds can also be caused by parasites, such as carp lice, leeches, and anchor worms. Fishes that have become weakened, perhaps through undernourishment, can easily be attacked by fungi. Winter is also a critical time. The temperature remains very low for long periods of time making goldfish more susceptible to fungal diseases. Affected skin areas have a "fluffy", cottonwool-like layer over them.

repeated 2 to 3 times if the first bath does not give the required result. You can also use Antimaladin, Mycopur, and Omnisan, which are available from aquarium and pet shops. These preparations are also used for the bathing or dipping of fishes or to be added to the pond or aquarium. Make sure the directions for use are strictly adhered to.

BACTERIA AND VIRUSES

Every aquarium and fish pond contains a multitude of

A rare telescope-eyed bluescale fringetail.

Treatment

Prepare a solution made up of 15 g salt (household grade) dissolved in 1 liter of water, and bathe the affected fish in it for 20 minutes. If need be, this treatment may have to be

bacteria that fulfill diverse tasks. Fishes are always in contact with them, but disease outbreaks occur only when the goldfish are weakened or wounds provide suitable settling sites for the bacteria. Different circumstances can trigger a disease outbreak: a change in environmental conditions, a deterioration of water quality, or a change in the health of the fish due to weakness, malnutrition, stress, etc.

Not all bacterial or viral diseases have characteristic symptoms which are easily recognizable by a beginning aquarist. Therefore, we have concentrated our discussion on two diseases which permit a definitive diagnosis. A fish that becomes clearly restless, moves off on its own, becomes apathetic, is unable to swim properly, always holds its fins tightly against the body, and gains or loses weight conspicuously, is sick. If the symptoms are very diffuse and unclear, and don't match any of the diseases so far described, then you should consult an experienced aquarium dealer or pet shop. With aimless applications of various medications you will probably kill the fish, which ordinarily could have been saved by a correct and specific treatment.

CARP POX
This disease occurs primarily during the colder period of the year, and so it's principally a problem confined to ponds and aquariums kept outdoors. It's also frequently

Some fish diseases are hard to detect in their beginning stages. Although this calico ryukin appears healthy in sight and activity, it could very well be infected with an internal parasite or non-visible bacterial infection.

found among goldfish kept in pools that are fed continuously by underground springs.

The name "carp pox" is somewhat misleading since it has nothing to do with pox, but is caused by a Herpes-like virus. Affected specimens

water is sometimes advantageous.

DROPSY

This is one of the more common diseases affecting carp-like fishes. Infected fishes have usually been stressed by poor

A close-up of the head region of a high quality hamanishiki.

show slimy, but solid skin elevations of various sizes on body and fins. The skin changes are reminiscent of a fungal disease. This disease usually lasts for several months. Generally, the affected fish don't convey the impression of being sick, having only moderately affected behavior. Mortalities are rare. There are no medications available in successfully treating this disease. Usually the disease disappears by itself, once the water temperature rises. Placing the fish into warmer

environmental conditions or have been poorly fed. There are several distinct symptoms indicating an infected fish. From one day to the next affected fish suddenly appear exhausted, display loss of equilibrium, and can easily be caught. The fish's body accumulates large amounts of fluid, the eyes begin to protrude from the head, and the scales are raised off the body. The fish often resembles a pine cone. In addition, there may be pus oozing out of the anal opening. Usually fish affected like this can not be

Facing
Page: A
magnificent
pair of gold
Chinese
lionheads.

saved and will often die within 1 to 2 days.

The chronic form of infectious dropsy extends over a long period of time, then disappears, and may suddenly break out again. The typical symptoms are hemorrhaging and often fungus-covered lesions. They're sometimes so deep that the bones and the digestive tract become visible. In contrast to the acute form, there may be a cure, provided early corrective action is taken.

On the basis of what has been said here about this disease, you will appreciate how important it is to initiate preventative measures for the well-being of your goldfish.

Chloramphenicol into the food at a dosage of 3 g per 1000 g of food. This fortified food should be given for 10 days to the entire fish population. It must be stressed that dropsy can be very difficult to cure and despite treatment will often cause the demise of your fish.

GILL ROT

This disease is also referred to as branchio-necrosis, and is strongly dependent upon environmental conditions. It occurs principally in ponds during the summer months when water temperatures are at their highest. Ponds that have abundant decaying organic matter provide ideal

Gill rot often forms in goldfish kept in outdoor ponds. The combination of warm water and decaying matter in the pond can provide the ideal setting for its development.

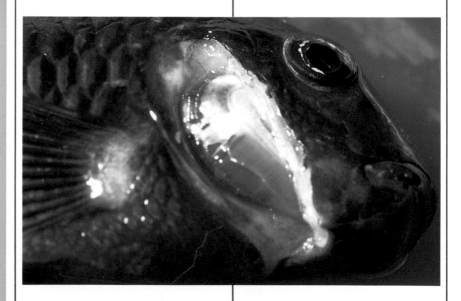

Treatment

Cyprinopur, a preparation available from aquarium shops, has proven to be very effective in many cases. For stubborn cases one can mix

conditions for the development of gill rot. The disease is caused by some of the lower fungi which grow into the veins of the gill sheets. This results in

This pearlscale is missing some scales on the body. Infection may be prevented with the use of appropriate medication.

Facing Page: A gorgeous red oranda.

stoppage of blood circulation through the gills. In the later stages, the gill sheets start to stop functioning, decay, and fall off. The fish is then no longer capable (or only in a limited way) of taking up oxygen from the water. Fishes affected in this matter will have difficulties breathing, which is easily recognized by the heavy pumping action of their gills, and their constant search for areas in the water that have a higher oxygen concentration, such as moving or inflowing water.

Treatment

Immediately stop feeding for at least 2 weeks in order to prevent a further build-up of waste products. The ailing fish may be treated with a salt bath. Each day about 1/3 of the water should be drained off and replaced with tap water. Make sure the filtration system is working properly.

TUMORS AND LESIONS

Goldfish can also be affected by tumors and lesions. However, it is often quite difficult to find out what the causes are. It's important to observe the fish closely and immediately take appropriate action when any of them display changes in body or skin. Early detection and treatment is best, because many tumors can be cured provided they are taken care of immediately and removed surgically. Never attempt operations of this magnitude by yourself, and consulting an experienced fish specialist is the smarter alternative.

INDEX

Anatomy, 68
Aquarium, 22
Aquarium, location of, 27-32
Aquarium, set-up, 25
Argulus foliaceus, 87
Black moor, 16, 70, 88
Body shape, 76
Bubble-eye, 16, 24
Bubble-eye, black, 17
Bubble-eye, calico, 52, 60
Carassius auratus, 6
Carassius auratus gibelio, 11
Carp Pox, 92
Celestial, 16, 71
Celestial, pom-pon, 77
Ceratophyllum, 44
Colors, 75
Comet, 13
Common goldfish, 7, 13
Cryptocoryne, 24
Dropsy, 93
Elodea, 24, 44
Eye shapes, 76
Fantail, 14
Fantails, calico, 14, 81, 84
Feeding, 62-66
Filtration, 46-50
Fins, 76
Food dispenser, 61
Garden pond, 32, 38, 40, 41
Garden pool, 35, 37
Gill rot, 94
Goldfish, breeding, 68
Goldfish, history of, 11
Hamanishiki, 93
Head shape, 78
Ich, 88
Leeches, 86
Lernaea cyprinacea, 87
Lesions, 96
Lionhead, 18
Lionhead, Chinese, 19, 78
Lionhead, golden, 95
Lionhead, red and white, 9
Lionhead, white, 72
Moor, broadtail, 76
Oranda, 5, 16

Oranda, black, 80
Oranda, black and red
    telescope-eye fringetail, 32
Oranda, calico, 12, 77
Oranda, lemon, 39
Oranda, pearlscale, 83
Oranda, pom-pon, 73
Oranda, red, 17, 51, 74, 81,
    97
Oranda, red and white, 23
Oranda, red-capped, 29
Ornamental koi, 31
Pearlscale, 19, 96
Pearlscale, calico, 18, 75
pH, 26
Ranchu, 18, 27
Ranchu, red, 8, 36
Ranchu, orange and white, 89
Ranchu, white and red, 49
Ryukin, calico, 43, 92
Ryukin, red and white, 15, 43
Sagittaria, 24
Saprolegnia, 90
Scales, 75
Sensory Organs, 74
Shubunkin, 14
Telescope-eye, 16, 66
Telescope-eye, bluescale
    fringetail, 91
Telescope-eye, calico
    butterflytail, 50, 82
Telescope-eye, orange pom-
    pon, 58
Telescope-eye, red and white,
    4, 85
Telescope-eye, red and white
    butterflytail, 79
Temperature, 55, 56
Tosakin, 15
Tub, 30
Tumors, 96
Vallisneria, 24
Veiltail, 7
Velvet, 88
Water, 34
Water conditioners, 54
Water lily, 4, 44